Grayson Morgan

Shifting the Security Paradigm

Grayson Morgan

Shifting the Security Paradigm

The Risks of Information Assurance

VDM Verlag Dr. Müller

Copyright © 2007 VDM Verlag Dr. Müller e. K. and licensors
All rights reserved. Saarbrücken 2007
Contact: info@vdm-verlag.de
Cover image: www.purestockx.com
Publisher: VDM Verlag Dr. Müller e. K., Dudweiler Landstr. 125 a, 66123 Saarbrücken, Germany
Produced by: Lightning Source Inc., La Vergne, Tennessee/USA
            Lightning Source UK Ltd., Milton Keynes, UK

Copyright © 2007 VDM Verlag Dr. Müller e. K. und Lizenzgeber
Alle Rechte vorbehalten. Saarbrücken 2007
Kontakt: info@vdm-verlag.de
Coverbild: www.purestockx.com
Verlag: VDM Verlag Dr. Müller e. K., Dudweiler Landstr. 125 a, 66123 Saarbrücken, Deutschland
Herstellung: Lightning Source Inc., La Vergne, Tennessee/USA
            Lightning Source UK Ltd., Milton Keynes, UK

ISBN: 978-3-8364-2739-5

DEDICATION

This book is dedicated to my family, without whom life would have no meaning.

TABLE OF CONTENTS

LIST OF FIGURES

LIST OF TABLES

Chapter 1

Introduction

With the adoption of the Network Centric Operations (NCO) doctrine and its focus on creating decision superiority through the use of a collaborative communications environment, the Department of Defense (DoD) has turned its sights towards the development of a single, networked information system to facilitate this goal. Known as the Global Information Grid (GIG), this next generation of standardized network architecture and information services will form the backbone of the DoD's plan to interconnect decision-makers in real time.

DoD Directive 8000.1 - *Management of DoD Information Resources and Information Technology* provides performance criteria covering the operation of information systems by requiring that accurate and consistent information shall be available to decision-makers so they can effectively execute the DoD mission. While tools such as the GIG will provide them with unprecedented data access and collaborative capabilities, the *Joint Battle Management Command and Control Roadmap* noted that even the best-designed architectures, software, and systems might be flawed in subtle ways. Unfortunately, lessons learned from recent military operations repeatedly show the existence of just such a flaw associated with authorized users injecting poor quality data into highly secure information systems and the obstacle this risk represents to the military decision-makers attempting to attain desired levels of operational effectiveness.

Problem Statement

Because of non-existent DoD policies governing the requirement for high quality operational data and the consequential migration of this responsibility towards limited quality assurance capability Information Assurance (IA) security processes, military decision-makers using networked information systems are exposed to the vulnerability of degraded system integrity. When this vulnerability originates from poor data quality, it has the ability to mimic failures of IA and contributes to the risk of decision-maker uncertainty, a risk that undermines the very purpose of IA: maintaining user trust.

There is a need to expand IA risk assessment criteria to evaluate the uncertainty associated with the threat from poor data quality and the vulnerability of degraded system integrity. Under current assessment criteria and restrictions inherent to IA definitions, poor data quality does not qualify as an Information Assurance threat despite the ability to produce an outcome identical to an IA failure. It is my belief that an IA risk assessment created to aid decision-makers in determining mitigation strategies must include *any* threat capable of negatively impacting the IA process.

Hypotheses

The research goal of this book is framed by the following hypothesis, which examines elements of observed and documented operational failures of DoD information system security processes under IA:

Poor data quality is a threat to Information Assurance security processes.

Problem Resolution

This book will describe the design, analysis, and implementation of enhanced risk assessment criteria specifically created to identify the threats and vulnerabilities of networked information systems used in military operations. Key elements of the problem resolution strategy include the use of Action Research (AR) methodology for quick and continuous research analysis and the Defense Information Assurance Certification and Accreditation Process (DIACAP), the follow-on to the DoD Information Technology Security Certification and

Accreditation Process (DITSCAP), as the vehicle for implementation. The transition of the DoD's IA enforcement mechanism from the paper-driven DITSCAP to the web-based DIACAP will provide a platform capable of integrating proposed risk assessment criteria.

Unique Contributions

The research in this book will highlight four outcomes demonstrating a definitive contribution to applied knowledge in information technology; the identification of inherent IA limitations, a method for analyzing IA in military operations, the validation of poor data quality as an IA threat, and an effective implementation process for IA risk assessment improvements.

Scope of Research

The basis for this book is to research an IA problem per the Department of Defense Information Assurance Scholarship Program (IASP). As such, the scope of this research is limited to poor data quality threats within Department of Defense information systems and the risk to IA experienced by decision-makers using these systems during military operations. This research is focused on revealing the relationships between decision-maker uncertainty, poor data quality, and IA for the purpose of risk mitigation.

Chapter 2

Understanding the Problem

The DoD publication *Multiservice Procedures for Joint Task Force Information Management* (JTF-IM) defines IM as those processes involved in the creation, collection, control, dissemination, storage, retrieval, protection, and destruction of data with the goal of providing quality data. Data quality is not measurable as a single attribute, but consists of multiple criteria to include accuracy, relevance, timeliness, usability, completeness, brevity, and security per Joint Publication 3-13 *Information Operations*. While decision-makers may place an emphasis on select characteristics and assign a weighted value based to situational need (i.e., accuracy may take priority over security), no single characteristic maintains a disproportionate influence on the overall measure of data quality.

Although the criteria of quality data identified to meet stringent military data requirements are listed in JTF-IM and JP 3-13, there is a pronounced lack of an enforcement mechanisms designed to prevent the compromise of these characteristics and this void contributes to the risk of decision-maker uncertainty. The unique status of security as the only operational DoD data quality criteria of the seven listed to be provided with mandated protections under U.S. Code in the form of the *Defense Information Assurance Program*, DoD Directive 8500.1 – *Information Assurance (IA)*, and DoD Instruction 8500.2 – *Information Assurance (IA) Implementation* not only speaks to IM priorities within the DoD, but also underscores a reliance on IA to maintain the other criteria of data quality for which there is no intent.

The importance of IA security protections to the achievement of DoD goals and objectives involving combat missions is reflected by the Mission Assurance Category (MAC) classification imbedded within DoD Instruction 8500.2. Primarily used to determine requirements for availability and integrity, MAC rankings of I (vital), II (important), or III (unnecessary in the short term) are assigned to each DoD Information System (IS), but those used in combat operations requiring high integrity automatically receive either a MAC I or II designation. The consequences surrounding a loss of integrity in a MAC I or II system could seriously impact mission effectiveness and are deemed unacceptable by the DoD.

Under existing conditions, authorized users of DoD information systems, both human and machine, have the ability to create inaccurate, irrelevant, untimely, unusable, incomplete, and unnecessary data which is routinely injected into otherwise secure information systems for use by decision-makers. Despite this sobering reality, IA does offer DoD a wide range of protection mechanisms to prevent and mitigate security related risks under the security services or five 'pillars' of availability, integrity, authentication, confidentiality, and non-repudiation.

However, one example of an IA threat not covered by an IA enforcement mechanism occurs when decision-makers acknowledge the existence of poor data quality within their secure information network, either through contradictory data or post-decision failure (i.e., shot at friendly forces, maneuvered in wrong direction, etc.). Such situations compel the decision-maker to ask: *Was this data simply flawed or was it maliciously altered?* The inability of security processes to prevent or mitigate the "illusion" of an integrity failure caused by poor data quality undermines the very purpose of IA – to enhance user trust in their networked information systems.

Limitations of IA

Definitions constitute the origin of IA limitations and in each case the imposed restrictions are intentional, although definitions for words such as risk assessment, threat, authorized user, integrity, and data integrity play an integral part in advancing the IA risk of decision-maker uncertainty. The official source of IA terms, known as the Committee on National Security Systems Instruction (CNSSI) No. 4009 – *National Information Assurance (IA) Glossary*, is referenced in numerous DoD directives, notices, and instructions covering the subjects of IA, IM, and DoD information systems.

The ability to mitigate risk, the possibility that a particular threat will adversely impact an IS by exploiting a particular vulnerability, is curtailed in the realm of IA due to restrictions in the Glossary. While a vulnerability is openly defined as a weakness in an IS, system security procedures, internal controls, or implementation that could be exploited, a threat is limited to any circumstance or event with the potential to adversely impact an IS through unauthorized access, destruction, disclosure, modification of data, and/or denial of service. As written, the *perception* of a threat is not classified as a threat even if the outcome has the potential to create an equally adversely impact or risk.

The definition of integrity, the most likely IA security service with ties to the threat of poor data quality, is clear on the lack of any relationship. Per the IA Glossary, integrity is the quality of an information system reflecting the logical correctness and reliability of the operating system; the logical completeness of the hardware and software implementing the protection mechanism; and the consistency of the data structures and occurrences of the stored data. (Note that, in a formal security mode, integrity is interpreted more narrowly to mean protection against unauthorized modification or destruction of information).

Based on this definition, integrity applies only to the quality of the information system, not the data within the information system. Data structures and occurrences are aspects of format and context having no connection to data characteristics. The attached note also discounts the degradation to integrity associated with poor data quality by excluding authorized users operating within their assigned authorities from creating such a threat, a direct contradiction to National Institute of Standards and Technology (NIST) findings of their Computer Systems Laboratory (CSL) (CSL Bulletin 1994). As such, degradation to integrity is termed a *dangling vulnerability* with no implied risk since the corresponding threat of poor data quality created by authorized users is not recognized.

Although not one of the five IA pillars, data integrity is similar to, but distinct from data quality (CSL Bulletin 1993). A subset of integrity, data integrity is defined by the Glossary as the condition existing when data is unchanged from its source and has not been accidentally or maliciously modified, altered, or destroyed. Like that of integrity and the disregard of quality characteristics at data generation, this definition allows inaccurate, irrelevant, untimely, unusable, incomplete, and unnecessary data the ability to carry the IA badge of integrity. The computer age axiom of GIGO – Garbage In, Garbage Out – (Fry and Sibley 1976) can now be extended to that of secure GIGO under IA.

Decision-Maker Misperceptions

Flawed perceptions regarding the capabilities of IA and its limitations has led to incorrect assumptions by DoD policy makers regarding their ability to expose information system risk caused by poor data quality and the vulnerability of integrity degradation. Errors can arise in defining and evaluating computer security policy as well as in translating that policy into procedures. The effect of such errors in policy upon the secure operation of information systems can impose unacceptable levels of risk from the perspective of procurers and users of information systems (Sibley et al. 1993).

Per the IA Glossary, a risk assessment is the process of analyzing threats to and vulnerabilities of an information system and the potential impact resulting from the loss of information or capabilities of a system. This definition implies all threats and vulnerabilities creating a negative impact on system capabilities, not just those concerning IA. Imprecision in policy definition contributes to the introduction of inconsistent, unintended, or unsound policies. Errors in the definition and evaluation of computer security policy become embedded in an information system if they are not detected and resolved prior to mapping policy to procedure (Sibley et al. 1993).

Those under a misperception also include the Congress of the United States. By law, a vulnerability and threat (i.e., risk) assessment of elements of the defense and supporting non-defense information infrastructures that are essential to the operations of the DoD is required under the *Defense Information Assurance Program* (United States Code, Title 10, Subtitle A, Part IV, Chapter 131, § 2224). Unbeknownst to members of Congress relying on this law to maintain DoD operations, the risk assessment implemented under DIACAP to enforce protection is limited by design to only IA defined vulnerabilities and threats. These and other flaws, errors of commission, omission, or oversight in an information system can allow protection mechanisms to be bypassed.

Chapter 3

Literature Research

Literature research was performed in two areas: the impact of data quality on networked

information systems, and the evolution of Information Assurance (IA) in the face of changing

practices and technology.

Impact of Data Quality

The impact of data quality on networked systems is well documented and ranges from

research confirming the high likelihood of inconsistencies in information systems as a result of

overlapping databases (Motro et. al. 2004), to the cascading effect of both data and application

problems within network centric environments (Khalilzad 1999, Kott et al. 2001, Bass and

Robichaux 2001). These studies confirmed that poor quality data and application failures linked

to such data not only migrate throughout a networked information system, but they also have a

multiplying effect leading to even greater problems than originally observed (Miller 2004). The

outcomes documented in this research include increased decision-maker uncertainty, a risk

highlighted as being a direct factor in reducing decision-maker accuracy (Kott et al. 2001).

As a vulnerability to information system security, quality data failures are documented so

frequently as to form entire IA domains linked to threats such as human induced errors, user

abuses of authority, and poor policy implementation (Baker 1993, Abrams et. al. 1995, Jonsson

et al. 1999, Bass and Robichaux 2001). Literature also indicates system users have a limited

capacity to detect such risk parameters, although the use of quality data incentives and risk

expectations from error rates have shown an ability to improve this capability (Davis et al. 1967,

Laudon 1986, Ricketts 1990, Kline 2000). Regardless of the source of the vulnerability or the threat capable of exploiting it, studies on the impact of data quality to user confidence highlight both the uncertainty risk present in the situational awareness of decision-makers and just how poorly calibrated user confidence is to actual data quality (CLS Bulletin 1994, Endsley 2003, Miller 2004).

Research in the field of data quality modeling shows that, like quality control in manufacturing, poor quality data has a cost associated with it that is best overcome by the building of quality controls directly into network centric processes (Readman 1995, Wang et. al. 1992). An important factor to consider in this regard is that data quality standards required by decision-makers are situational and often in conflict with each other (Fry and Sibley 1976, Labbe 1999, Arnborg et al. 2000). When this is the case, it is recommended decision-makers specify the quality data characteristics most important to them in the context of their environment and mission requirements (Haxen 2004).

Evolution of Information Assurance

The fortress model of IA currently underpinning most DoD security processes is rooted in the historic assumptions that information systems are closed and under central administrative control, but such a model is only as strong as its weakest component. Once the security wall is breached, the entire network is at risk. Research indicates decision-makers can no longer be content with this traditionally defined technical approach to information security as a broader view of IA is required to take into account socio-technical design methods (Strens and Dobson 1993, Schneider 1998, Bellocci et al. 2001). The assumption that security is absolute is another area in need of replacement with a mechanism to lets decision-makers know how much confidence they are justified in having with regard to their networked information systems as existing policies do not provide complete – 100% effective – information security (Sibley et al.1993, Wulf et al.1995, Blakley 1996).

The need to redefine IA processes covering information systems has also been the subject of much debate. Recent work promotes risk management as a paradigm to allow for fail-soft and fail-safe mechanisms demanded by military operations where the cost of even the smallest margin of error or mission failure is unacceptably high (Skitka et al. 1999, Lipson and Fisher 1999). In this IA model, security services protect the mission of the decision-maker, not the information system being utilized, and IA implementation policy forms an essential link between risk mitigation and mission accomplishment (NIST Special Publication 800-53). Risk assessments are a vital tool in achieving baseline performance measures needed to achieve such endeavors.

Studies endorsing the evolution of the security paradigm from fortress to risk based indicate how the IA pillar of integrity is based on decision-maker trust and includes the quality data characteristics of accuracy, relevancy, and completeness as yardsticks for risk mitigation of IA vulnerabilities (Motro 1987, Maconachy 2001). Maintaining decision-maker trust and confidence in information systems is at the uppermost level of concern in operational military environments and one of the most difficult to measure (Bisantz et al. 1999). To do this, researchers suggest the characteristics of system trustworthiness not be evaluated individually, but as a whole to ensure one is not satisfied at the expense of others (Schneider 1998). This premise is based on the fact past information networks were closed systems with data coming from a single source and users learning to trust it by experience or intuition. With the origin of data in networked information systems so complex, it makes intuition useless (Cooper 1994, Arnborg et al. 2000, Cummings 2004).

Chapter 4

Background to DIACAP

Implemented as a replacement to the fortress model based DITSCAP, DoD Instruction

8510.bb – *DoD Information Assurance Certification and Accreditation Process (DIACAP)*

reflects the risk based assessment required during ongoing transformation of DoD information

technology, legislation under the *Federal Information Security Management Act* (FISMA), IA

policies outlined in DoD Directive 8500.1 and DoD Instruction 8500.2, and the adoption of the

network centric GIG architecture. According to 8500.2, all elements of a DoD information

system IA program shall be developed, implemented, and maintained through the DIACAP and

it shall be the mechanism for negotiating IA requirements and capabilities.

DoD designed this Certification and Accreditation (C&A) process to take a risk

management approach to IA by balancing information important to mission accomplishment

against documented threats and vulnerabilities. **Figure 1** shows how work within the DIACAP

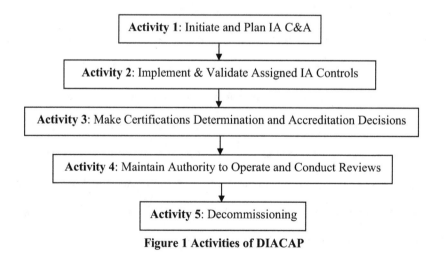

Figure 1 Activities of DIACAP

is divided into five activities, with each activity tasked to achieve a specific certification and accreditation output.

Activity 1 – *Initiate and Plan IA C&A* – begins with each DoD information system being assigned one of nine baseline IA levels drawn from the nine independent combinations of MAC (I, II, or III) and confidentiality level (classified, sensitive, or public information) that may coexist within the GIG. **Table 1** shows these combinations and their associated IA Controls.

Per the 8500.2 instruction, these baseline IA levels are achieved by applying a specified set of IA Controls to the system with each control describing an objective IA condition that is testable, where compliance is measurable, and the activities required to achieve the IA Control are assigned and accountable.

Table 1 MAC and Confidentiality Levels (DoD Instruction 8500.2)

Mission Assurance Category and Confidentiality Level	Applicable IA Controls
MAC I, Classified	Attachments A1 and A4
MAC I, Sensitive	Attachments A1 and A5
MAC I, Public	Attachments A1 and A6
MAC II, Classified	Attachments A2 and A4
MAC II, Sensitive	Attachments A2 and A5
MAC II, Public	Attachments A3 and A6
MAC III, Classified	Attachments A3 and A4
MAC III, Sensitive	Attachments A3 and A5
MAC III, Public	Attachments A3 and A6

IA Controls

As defined in DoD 8500.1, an IA control is an objective IA condition of integrity, availability or confidentiality achieved through the application of specific safeguards or through the regulation of specific activities expressed in a specified format (i.e., control subject area, control number, control name, and control text). **Figure 2** is an example of the IA Control

format for the objective IA conditions of integrity and availability.

IA Control Subject Area: Security Design and Configuration
IA Control Number: DCSQ-1
IA Control Name: Software Quality
IA Control Text: Software quality requirements and validation methods that are
focused on the minimization of flawed or malformed software that can negatively
impact integrity or availability are specified for all software development initiatives.

Figure 2 IA Control

Table 2 shows the breakdown of the 157 unique IA Controls into the 8 subject areas.

The IA control number is a unique identifier with the first two letters an abbreviation for the

subject area name and the second two are an abbreviation for the individual IA Control name.

Table 2 Subject Areas (DoD Instruction 8500.2)

Abbreviation	Subject Area Name	Number of Controls in Subject Area
DC	Security Design & Configuration	31
IA	Identification and Authentication	9
EC	Enclave and Computing Environment	48
EB	Enclave Boundary Defense	8
PE	Physical and Environmental	27
PR	Personnel	7
CO	Continuity	24
VI	Vulnerability and Incident Management	3

The number (1, 2 or 3) represents a level of robustness in ascending order relative to the control.

If the number is a 2, there is a 1 with less robustness and there may be a 3 offering more. **Figure**

3 shows an example of IA Control numbering.

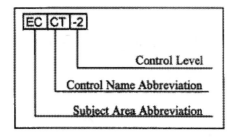

Figure 3 IA Control Numbering (DoD Instruction 8500.2)

DIACAP Activity 2 – *Implement & Validate Assigned IA Controls* – contains the core certification analysis tasks required to validate the current environment against identified IA Controls. One of these tasks is a vulnerability assessment to evaluate each of the five IA security pillars and identify any residual risks, that portion of risk remaining after required IA Controls are applied.

Activity 3 – *Make Certification Determination & Accreditation Decisions* – analyzes identified residual risks using calculations based on the likelihood of occurrence, the rationale used to accept or reject such risks, and operational impacts before issuing the certification and making an accreditation decision.

Although countermeasures are recommended to reduce residual risk, this becomes a moot point regarding the vulnerability of degraded system integrity and the threat of poor data quality as no IA Control or subject area exists to protect the high integrity requirements of MAC I and II designated systems from this particular risk of decision-maker uncertainty.

Activity 4 – *Maintaining Authority to Operate and Conduct Reviews* – initiates and updates the lifecycle implementation plan for IA Controls. Regular reviews of system vulnerabilities and annual assessments are required to maintain situational awareness and needed IA posture.

Activity 5 – *Decommissioning* – conducts activities related to the disposition of DIACAP registration information and system related data in GIG supporting IA infrastructure and core enterprise services.

Chapter 5

Methodology

The method followed for conducting this qualitative research was the collection and

analysis of data in support of an exploratory research study. The primary sources of data

originate from Government Accounting Office (GAO) reports to Congress from 1998-2004 and

military lessons learned reports regarding *Operation Enduring Freedom* (OEF) and *Operation*

Iraqi Freedom (OIF) activities from 2001-2002.

Research Plan

Selection of a research technique to facilitate an applied risk assessment involving data

quality was the first stage in the overall design. While a variety of research methods are

recognized by the information systems community under the two main techniques of quantitative

or theory driven (i.e., survey, laboratory experiments, formal, and numerical) and qualitative or

data driven (i.e., action research, case study, and ethnography) (Myers 1997), the characteristics

of qualitative research best compliment the project objective. These characteristics include:

- Data gathering usually tied to less structured research instruments

- Findings that are more in-depth since they make greater use of open-ended questions

- Results providing much more detail on behavior, attitudes and motivation

- Research that is more intensive and flexible

- Results based on smaller sample sizes and are often not representative of the
  population

- Research that may not be easily replicated or repeated, giving it low reliability

- Analysis of results seen as much more subjective (Joppe 2005).

The socio-technical nature of the project objectives also played an important role in identifying an effective research method, but other key factors arise from the Engineer Degree in Information Technology program. The most important aspects of this program are the requirements for a definitive contribution to applied knowledge in information technology and the completion of an applied project. Taking these variables into consideration made Action Research (AR) a compelling method upon which to establish a project design.

Action Research

AR was originally developed within the social sciences as a collaborative effort between researchers and practitioners (sometimes one in the same) for the purpose of testing specific interventions on a perceived problem. In social settings, this method allows for feedback obtained from such interventions to be rapidly filtered back into the process as a controlled change to re-evaluate a hypothesis. This constant insertion of feedback provides rapid evaluation, correction, and improvement to socially driven processes of human interaction. Recent high impact integrations of information technology into social processes have proven this method increasingly useful at exploring the complexities of information systems within organizational contexts.

As a dual-purpose research method focused on both process improvement and knowledge creation, AR utilizes the five-stage cycle of *diagnosing* (identify or define a problem), *action planning* (consider courses of action for solving a problem), *action taking* (select a course of action), *evaluation* (study the consequences of the action), and *specified learning* (identify general findings) to study small samples of an organizational problem in great detail (Susman and Evered 1978). **Figure 4** illustrates the continuing evolution of the AR process as researchers repeat the cycle until an outcome is reached.

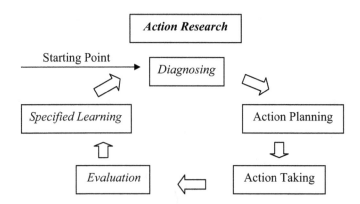

Figure 4 Action Research Cycle

Researchers found numerous benefits from AR in the risk analysis of information systems by utilizing a modified five-stage cycle (Baskerville and Stage 2000). **Figure 5** illustrates this new process. Although similar to the original social sciences model, these stages focus specifically on the risks analysis process and are reminiscent of systems engineering development cycles (i.e., waterfall, spiral, etc.) used in software and technology (Sage 1992, 1999).

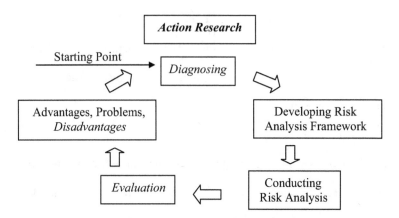

Figure 5 Risk Analysis Action Research Cycle

In this research, the AR for risk analysis methodology is used for:

Diagnosing – the impact of data quality based risk documented in GAO reports and the

lessons learned from operational military units.

Developing Risk Analysis Framework – from Activity 2 – *Implement & Validate*

Assigned IA Controls in the DIACAP to reduce the risk of data

quality based uncertainty.

Conducting Risk Analysis – of the systems highlighted by the GAO and in lessons learned

by utilizing Activity 3 – *Make Certifications Determination and*

Accreditation Decision in the DIACAP.

Evaluation – of differences between the DIACAP and the need for modifications due to

unacceptable residual risks.

Advantages, Disadvantages, Problems – of implementing modifications to the DIACAP.

Diagnosing – 1st Stage

Utilization of the AR risk analysis cycle provides two distinct opportunities for

qualitative data collection. The first involves the starting point in the cycle where diagnosing of

a problem begins with the collection and review of documents such as GAO reports created at

the request of Congress and military lessons learned. While a qualitative research approach such

as this cannot answer questions of *how often* or *how many*, it can give indications of *why*, *how*, or

when an event occurs (Joppe 2005).

GAO Reports

GAO/NSIAD-98-73 C4I Interoperability – A GAO/National Security and International

Affairs Division report documented poor quality data in an uncertified Command, Control,

Communications, Computers, Intelligence (C4I) system due to data exchange problems that

resulted in the simulated downing of a commercial airplane during a joint exercise. Also highlighted were the Joint Tactical Information Distribution System (JTIDS) and the Air Defense System Integrator (ADSI), secure systems which contained so much poor quality data due to data exchange problems that real world use would have resulted in death of numerous pilots and friendly systems being attacked.

GAO-03-329 Intelligence System Interoperability – This report documented how only 2 of 26 Distributed Common Ground-Surface Systems (DCGS) designed to process intelligence data (reconnaissance, radar systems, satellites, remote ground sensors, and electronic signals) had certifications establishing system confidentiality and integrity. At the time of the report, 21 of the non-certified systems were in operational military use. The GAO found there was a greater risk due to the inability of these systems to share data in a timely manner and that some of them were critical to the success of other intelligence systems (cascading failure).

GAO-04-547 Communications Technology – This investigation reported that the Joint Targeting Cycle used by decision-makers in combat during network centric operations is highly dependent on the quality of interactions among the people and systems involved. Limitations reported during operations in Afghanistan included difficulties due to the unreliability of secure communications and data exchange processes subject to error.

GAO-04-858 Global Information Grid – The report identified IA as one of the most critical challenges facing the DoD with web based GIG systems exposed to the same vulnerabilities of poor quality data that face all users of the Internet. It went on to state that both network centric warfare and GIG objectives present enormous challenges given the size of the network and the thousands of systems and users that will be linked to it. The report highlights how these risks will require significant changes in DoD culture regarding information systems.

Lessons Learned

Successful risk analysis of data quality vulnerability in the DoD's information system environment can only be achieved if the context for conducting the analysis is part of the answer. In the six month period between May and October of 2003, thousands of hours of observation, over 600 interviews with personnel engaged in operations, and more than 80 gigabytes of situational data provided the analysts at Joint Forces Command with a snapshot of combat operations information usage and effectiveness in the form of lessons learned during *Operation Enduring Freedom* (OEF) and *Operation Iraqi Freedom* (OIF). **Figure 6** shows how the increase of information bandwidth available to the military decision-maker in these operations compares with the similar conflict only 12 years earlier.

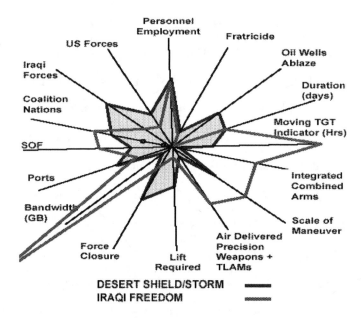

Figure 6 Comparisons of Warfare (JLL 2003)

While the bandwidth of the network centric information environment provided considerable increase in the effectiveness of certain combat capabilities (combined arms, precision weapons, etc.), the quality of the decisions and the network centric processes used to achieve the desired goals repeatedly showed signs weakness. According to the commander of U.S. Joint Forces Command, enhanced information system capabilities demonstrated severe limitations and a need for substantial improvements.

Due to changes in decision-making processes such as the reduced timeframe, increased numbers of network users, and vast amounts of available data, vulnerabilities such as poor quality data became even more profound when they are incorporated into the ultra-dynamic environment of the tactical battlefront. The impacts of poor quality data vulnerability in secure information systems during military operations are reported in lessons learned below.

1ˢᵗ Marine Division (May 2003) – Widespread use of the Secret Internet Protocol Router Network (SIPRNET) by authorized users to propagate poor quality data resulted in a *loss of faith* by commanders and created *confusion and fear* that was unnecessary. Multiple versions of overlays and human error in the Command and Control Personal Computer (C2PC) created *confusion* at all levels. Decision-makers were inundated with intelligence information and data that had little bearing on their mission or requirements. There was also *little confidence* in the Modernized Integrated Database (MIDB) to provide general military intelligence, as it was often *untrustworthy* and resulted in decision-makers choosing a periodic quality-controlled product over real-time erroneous information.

US Army Air Defense Artillery Quality Assurance Office (September 2003) – Poor quality data created by the PATRIOT anti-air missile system and injected into the network degraded the overall air picture to the point where decision-maker *uncertainty* over safety of flight became an issue and PATRIOT data was dropped despite being the only system capable of countering the threat of SCUD ballistic missiles.

Marine Corps Systems Command Liaison Team (April 2003) – Communicators, operations officers, and commanders routinely operated in *information overload* as they received information over too many different networks. Statements on the Data Automated Communications Terminal (DACT) used to track force locations suggest low decision-maker confidence due to *poor reliability*. Some instances reported units showing up in the wrong country or appearing miles away from their known locations.

2nd Brigade, 101st Airborne Division (AASLT) (2003) - The Blue Force Tracker (BFT) was unable to provide true unit locations for decision-makers and rarely made data reported through the chain of command accurate or timely.

3rd Infantry Division (July 2003) – Data used by decision-makers on secure Remote Workstations (RWS) became an inaccurate portrayal of the enemy situation. Secure communications available to the Intelligence Battlefield Operating System (IBOS) during OIF were insufficient to ensure timely, accurate, and relevant intelligence dissemination across the entire battlefield. Many secure intelligence systems were incapable of exchanging data with each other and those that could proved *unreliable*.

Center for Army Lessons Learned (October 2003) - As decision-makers had to monitor multiple systems (up to seven) during combat operations and input data manually, the risk of *uncertainty* caused by human error increased dramatically.

Developing Risk Analysis Framework – 2nd Stage

This stage of the AR process is achieved through the use of the Activity 2 - *Implement & Validate Assigned IA Controls* under DIACAP. The vulnerability assessment required by

Activity 2 includes the identification of any residual risks as a result of documented vulnerabilities and associated threats after IA Controls have been applied. With the current implementation of IA Controls required for MAC I and II systems in place, no residual risks resulting from the repeated incidents of poor data quality vulnerability were identified.

In reality, implemented IA Controls are unable to mitigate repeated and widespread risk of uncertainty created by poor data quality. This is not due to the weakness of any single or group of IA Controls, but the outright lack of any IA control for the IA threat of poor data quality.

Conducting Risk Analysis – 3rd Stage

The third AR stage provides the other opportunity for qualitative data collection by analyzing the risks identified in the previous stage. Like the 2nd Stage, the 3rd Stage also corresponds to a DIACAP activity and in this instance the alignment is with Activity 3 – *Make Certification Determination & Accreditation Decisions*. Using calculations based on the likelihood of occurrence, the rationale used to accept or reject such risks, and any operational impacts they create, a risk analysis is completed prior to issuing the system certification and making an accreditation decision. With no residual risks identified comprising of both an official IA vulnerability and an official IA threat, all of the systems identified as having data quality issues were certified and given accreditation to operate.

In reality, the lack of IA Controls for poor data quality created significant and well documented residual risks: loss of [system] faith, confusion and fear, little confidence, information overload, and uncertainty. All of which create unacceptable outcomes. No rationale is given for the acceptance of these uncertainty risks within the DoD operational IS environment despite a documented inability to meet DoD requirements for data quality and the integrity mandate for MAC I and II systems.   The lack of comprehensive statistical data on this threat to

IA makes it nearly impossible to evaluate the likelihood of risk occurrence as DoD entities such

as the Defense Information Systems Agency (DISA), the agency responsible for GIG criteria and

operations, disavow responsibility for maintaining data quality standards and commands like the

U.S. Joint Forces Command (USJFCOM) Joint Futures Laboratory (JFL) with state-of-the-art

operational testing facilities do not keep metrics for data quality in a networked DoD information

system and have never intentionally evaluated the impact of poor quality data on military

operations.

Evaluation – 4th Stage

All of the systems identified from the 1st stage of AR were MAC I or II systems in which

an implied loss of integrity had seriously impacts on mission effectiveness, a condition deemed

unacceptable by the DoD. Given that the IA Controls of DoD Instruction 8500.2 were in effect

prior to all but one of the reports, we can conclude there is a flaw in the certification and

accreditation process as an unacceptable outcome is observed, but no IA Controls are authorized

to mitigate it. As such, it would appear that previous system C&As were done in error and

should be revoked prior to all DoD information systems being reevaluated under more stringent

IA Controls.

The DoD rationale to ignore poor data quality as an IA threat is unclear given the

similarities between DIACAP and the government security controls found in NIST Special

Publication (SP) 800-53 – *Recommended Security Controls for Federal Systems*. SP 800-53

contains 163 security controls in 17 subject areas vice the 157 IA Controls in eight subject areas

found in the DIACAP. **Table 3** shows the full listing of the NIST security controls by class,

family, and identifier.

One of the NIST security controls under the operational family of System and Information (SI) Integrity is specifically designed to mitigate the threat of poor data quality: SI-10 – *Information Input Accuracy, Completeness, and Validity*. This security

Table 3 NIST Security Control Class, Family, and Identifiers (SP-800-53)

CLASS	FAMILY	IDENTIFIER
Management	Risk Assessment	RA
Management	Planning	PL
Management	System and Services Acquisition	SA
Management	Certification, Accreditation, and Security Assessments	CA
Operational	Personnel Security	PS
Operational	Physical and Environmental Protection	PE
Operational	Contingency Planning	CP
Operational	Configuration Management	CM
Operational	Maintenance	MA
Operational	System and Information Integrity	SI
Operational	Media Protection	MP
Operational	Incident Response	IR
Operational	Awareness and Training	AT
Technical	Identification and Authentication	IA
Technical	Access Control	AC
Technical	Audit and Accountability	AU
Technical	System and Communications Protection	SC

control has no counterpart in DIACAP. **Figure 7** details SI-10. Given this precedent of Federal government security controls for vulnerabilities beyond those contained in the DIACAP, the

---

Control: The information system checks information inputs for accuracy, completeness, and validity.

Supplemental Guidance: Checks for accuracy, completeness, and validity of information should be accomplished as close to the point of origin as possible. Rules for checking the valid syntax of information system inputs (e.g., character set, length, numerical range, acceptable values) are in place to ensure that inputs match specified definitions for format and content. Inputs passed to interpreters should be prescreened to ensure the content is not unintentionally interpreted as commands. The extent to which the information system is able to check the accuracy, completeness, and validity of information inputs should be guided by organizational policy and operational requirements.

**Figure 7 Security Control SI-10 – Information Input
Accuracy, Completeness, and Validity (SP-800-53)**

creation of a new IA Control based on the NIST security control of SI-10 becomes a possible solution. Using the format for IA Controls, details of SI-10 can be configured to meet the requirements of DIACAP. Additional guidance on the choice of control subject area placement can be derived from the IA Control for *Software Quality* in the Security Design and Configuration area, the only other IA Control with ties to quality. **Figure 8** provides an example of this new data quality based IA Control.

IA Control Subject Area: Security Design and Configuration
IA Control Number: DCDQ-2
IA Control Name: Data Quality
IA Control Text: Checks for accuracy, relevance, timeliness, usability, completeness, brevity, and security of data should be accomplished as close to the point of origin as possible. Rules for checking the valid syntax of information system inputs (e.g., character set, length, numerical range, acceptable values) are in place to ensure that inputs match specified definitions for format and content. Inputs passed to interpreters should be prescreened to ensure the content is not unintentionally interpreted as commands. The extent to which the information system is able to check data quality should be guided by organizational policy and operational requirements.

Figure 8 IA Control for Quality Data

Advantages, Disadvantages, Problems – 5th Stage

The final stage in the risk analysis AR cycle evaluates any proposed modifications to the DIACAP to determine the advantages achieved in doing so, the disadvantages associated with the change, and any additional problems that may arise. In the context of the poor quality data examples identified in the GAO reports and military lessons learned, incorporating a new IA Control for data quality offers several advantages as current standards, or lack there of, are incapable of mitigating and such threat. The main reason for the unacceptable system behaviors in three of the four GAO reports researched (98-73, 03-329, and 04-547) and all eight of the lessons learned referenced was poor data quality.

From a decision-maker perspective, an advantage of having an IA Control for data quality would be the acknowledgment of poor data quality as an IA threat instead of users being forced to operate under the paradoxical pretext that all information systems provide perfect data. While this control is unlikely to create perfect data just as DIACAP is unlikely to create perfectly secure data, decision maker awareness of actual risk and the knowledge that a process is in place to assess that risk solidifies the foundation of IA to promote user trust. Other advantages may exist, but their measures are best attained after the initiation of the proposed IA Control and future iterations of the AR cycle.

Disadvantages and problems from the creation of an IA Control dedicated to data quality are many. The most difficult hurdle to overcome will simply be imbedding the control into the DIACAP, which means updating the list of IA Controls in DoD Directive 8500.2. This may sound like a trivial exercise, but despite the knowledge of data quality risks to IA outlined in this book and ongoing efforts between DoD and the Intelligence Community to transition to NIST security controls, those responsible for such changes within the DoD Chief Information Officer's (CIO) Information Assurance office are unlikely to recommend such changes.

Why would the DoD CIO intentionally avoid both the responsibility and the opportunity to provide decision makers with policy changes that would reduce IA risk? While there are indications that a few individuals in the IA office acknowledge some level of risk originating from poor data quality, the actual driving force to prevent the adoption of a control to mitigate this risk is a combination of both an irrational belief that adoption of such a control would make IA responsible for DoD data quality and a desire to avoid the extra effort associated with this belief. By definition this is a moot argument as the IA Glossary states that information owners have the "responsibility for establishing the controls for [data] generation, collection, processing, dissemination, and disposal." An IA Control for data quality would simply serve to mandate implementation and also require it's incorporation into risk assessments.

Even if changes to IA Controls were made, the burdensome process of updating DoD instructions to keep pace with technological change is also a distinct disadvantage. NIST Special Publication-800-53 – *Recommended Security Controls for Federal Information Systems* has had 50 modifications since its release in February of 2005 easily inserted due to its web-based status; however, DoD directives and publications can go years or decades without changes despite being severely outdated (e.g., Joint Publication 6-0 *Doctrine for Command, Control, Communications, and Computer (C4) Systems Support to Joint Operations* – 30-May-95 was last updated in 2006). The DIACAP may be easier to use as a web-based process, but the IA Controls come from a signed DoD instruction.

Another significant disadvantage is that the inclusion of poor data quality as a threat to IA is a contradiction to the entrenched DoD security paradigm containing no reference to data quality. Just because something is true does not mean it will be easily accepted. Like the measures for specific advantages, disadvantages will also require continued iterations of the AR cycle to be properly evaluated.

Chapter 6

Conclusions and Future Work

The failure of the Department of Defense to evaluate the effects of poor data quality in networked information systems and take action to mitigate the impact of such conditions on critical military operations and decision-making is an unexplainable oversight in need of immediate correction. The unique risks of network centric operations involving the Global Information Grid and the continued reliance by decision makers on limited and unfamiliar Information Assurance practices to enforce non-existent data quality policies have led to dangerous and deadly consequences for military decision-makers.

The DoD Information Assurance program is tailored specifically to the data quality criteria of security and in a limited fashion. As the only data quality criteria enforced by law within the U.S. government, information system users improperly transfer responsibilities of data quality control to IA processes for which it has no mandate or capability.

The intentionally limited data quality capabilities of the IA program are in direct defiance of both a substantial body of academic research and the recommendations of government agency such as the General Accounting Office and the National Institute of Standards and Technology. Qualitative evidence from numerous sources document the unacceptable results of operating combat systems with poor quality data. In both exercises and real world use, these systems proved fallible to poor data quality induced decision failure.

Continued research into the effects of data quality in DoD networked information systems should be instituted to establish baselines for measuring change. As recommendations are implemented in the IA program or DIACAP, the quantitative and qualitative effects of each change have a bearing on future process improvement recommendations.

Without broader IA Controls to address areas of weakness within DIACAP, no amount of IA security program support or technical development will satisfy end user requirements for quality data. The value of quality data goes beyond the proper operation of the information system and extends to the user engaged in decision-making processes. It is essential for decision makers to understand the difference between IA security and data quality, as many believe the two are interchangeable. They are not and continued belief as such by anyone in the Department of Defense will increase the problematic assumption that data within a secure information network is of high quality simply because it is protected.

REFERENCES

Abrams, M. "Trusted System Concepts," *Computers & Security*, Vol. 14, No. 1, 1995, pp. 45-56.

Abrams, M., Jajodia, S., and Podell, Editors. *Information Security: An Integrated Collection of Essays*, IEEE Computer Society Press, Loss Alamitos, CA 1995.

Abrams, M. and Toth, P., Editors. *A Head Start on Assurance*, Proceeding of an Invitational Workshop on Information Technology (IT) Assurance and Trustworthiness, Williamsburg, Virginia, 21-23 March 19994.

Alberts, D. "Information Age Transformation," *Command and Control Research Program Publication*, Revision June 2002.

Alberts, D. and Hayes, R. "Power to the Edge: Command Control in the Information Age," *Command and Control Research Program Publication*, 2003.

Alberts, D., Garstka, J., Stein, F. "Network Centric Warfare," *Command and Control Research Program Publication*, February 2000.

Alberts, D., Garstka, J., Hayes, R. and Signori, D. "Understanding Information Age Warfare," *Command and Control Research Program Publication*, 2001.

Alexander, P. *Teamwork, Time, Trust and Information*, Proceedings of SAICSIT 2002, pp. 65-74.

Anokhin, P. and Motro, A. *Fusionplex: Resolution of Data Inconsistencies in the Integration of Heterogeneous Information Sources*, International Workshop on Information Quality in Information Systems, Paris, France, June 2004.

Avison, D., Lau, F., Myers, M. and Nielsen, P. "Action Research," *Communications of the ACM*, Vol. 42, No. 1, January 1999, pp. 94-97.

Baker, D. "The Evolved Threat Paradigm: Look Who's Wearing the Black Hats!," *ACM*, 1993, pp. 126-130.

---------. *Fortresses Built Upon Sand*, ACM New Security Paradigms Workshop, Lake Arrowhead, California, 1996.

Baskerville, R., and Stage, J. "Discourses on The Interaction of Information Systems, Organizations and Society: Reformation and Transformation," *Organizational and Social Perspectives on Information Technology*, Kluwer, Boston, 2000, pp. 1-12.

Baskerville, R., and Stage, J. *Organizational and Social Perspectives on Information Technology*, IFIP TC8 G8.2 International Working Conference on the Social and Organizational Perspective on Research and Practice in Information Technology, Aalborg, Denmark, 9-11 June, 2000.

Bass, T. and Robichaux, R. *Defense-In-Depth Revisited: Qualitative Risk Analysis Methodology for Complex Network-Centric Operations*, IEEE MILCOM 2001.

Bellocci, T., Ang, C., Ray, P., and Nof, S. *Information Assurance in Networked Enterprises: Definition, Requirements, And Experimental Results*, CERIAS Technical Report 2001-34, Research Memo School of Industrial Engineering No. 01-05, Purdue University, 2001.

Blakley, B. *The Emperor's Old Armor*, ACM New Security Paradigms Workshop, Lake Arrowhead, California, 1996.

Boehm, B. and In, H. "Identifying Quality-Requirement Conflicts," *IEEE Software*, March 1996.

Bolstad, C. and Endsley, M. *Shared Mental Models and Shared Displays: An Empirical Evaluation of Team Performance*, Proceedings of the 43rd Meeting of the Human Factors & Ergonomics Society, 1999.

Bouzeghoub, M. and Peralta, V. "A Framework for Analysis of Data Freshness," *ACM*, 2004, pp. 59-67.

Briefing on Joint Lessons Learned from Army Fellows Conference, 31 July 2003.

Briefing on Joint Lessons Learned to the U.S. House Armed Services Committee, 2 October 2003.

Burn, J. and Ma, L. *Integrating Business and IS Concepts Through Action Research Within a New IS Curriculum*, ACM, 1996, pp. 114-124.

Cappiello, C., Francalanci, C. and Pernici, B. "Data quality assessment from the user's prospective," *ACM*, 2004, pp. 68-73.

Cedilnik, A. and Rheingans, P. *Procedural Annotation of Uncertain Information*, IEEE, 2001, pp. 77-84.

Center for Army Lessons Learned. http://call.army.mil accessed on 15 March 2006.

Cheng, R. and Prabhakar, S. *Managing Uncertainty in Sensor Databases*, SIGMOD Record, vol. 32, No. 4, December 2003, pp. 41-46.

Committee on National Security Systems. *National Information Assurance (IA) Glossary.* Instruction No. 4009. Washington, D.C.: United States Government, May 2003.

Defense Information Systems Agency (DISA) presentation at Joint Systems Integration
     Command (JSIC), 17 November 2004.

Denning, D. and Denning, P. "Data Security," *Computing Surveys*, Vol. 11, No. 3,
     September 1979, pp. 227-249.

Department of Defense. *Department of Defense Information Technology Security
     Certification and Accreditation Process (DITSCAP)*. Application Manual 8501.1-M.
     Washington, D.C.: United States Government, 31 July 2000.

---------. *Doctrine for Battlespace Communication System (BCS) Support to Joint Operations*.
     Washington, D.C.: United States Government, 2 July 2004.

---------. *DoD Information Technology Security Certification and Accreditation Process
     (DITSCAP)*. Instruction 5200.40. Washington, D.C.: United States Government, 30
     December 1997.

---------. *DoD Net-Centric Data* Strategy. Memorandum. Washington, D.C.: United States
     Government, 9 May 2003.

---------. *Information Assurance (IA)*. Directive 8500.1. Washington, D.C.: United States
     Government, 24 October 2002.

---------. *Information Assurance (IA) Implementation*. Directive 8500.2. Washington, D.C.:
     United States Government, 6 February 2003.

---------. *Joint Battle Management Command and Control Roadmap – Version 2.0*.
     Washington, D.C.: United States Government, 27 February 2004.

---------. *Management of DoD information Resources and Information Technology*. Directive
     8000.1. Washington, D.C.: United States Government, 20 March 2002.

Department of Defense. *Multiservice Procedures for Joint Task Force Information
     Management (JFT-IM)*. Washington, D.C.: United States Government, April 1999.

---------. *Security Requirements for Automated Information Systems (AISs)*. Directive 5200.28.
     Washington, D.C.: United States Government, 21 March 1988.

Department of Defense Chief Information Officer (CIO). *DoD Net-Centric Data Strategy*.
     Washington, D.C.: United States Government, 9 May 2003.

Eloff, J. and Eloff, M. *Information Security Management – A New Paradigm*, Proceeding of
     SAICSIT, 2003, pp. 130-136.

Endsley, M. *Supporting Assessments of Uncertainty in Complex Worlds*, XVth International
     Ergonomics Association Triennial Congress, Seoul, Korea, August 2003, pp. 1.

Endsley, M. et. al. *Modeling and Measuring Situational Awareness in the Infantry Operational Environment*, U. S. Army Research Institute for the Behavioral and Social Sciences, October 1999.

Endsley, M. and Jones, W. *Situational Awareness Information Dominance & Information Warfare*, United States Air Force Armstrong Laboratory Technical Report AL/CF-TR-1997-0156, February 1997.

Funk, J., Chairperson. *Information Management and Data Quality*, Panel 1 discussion on Federal Data Quality Issues at the Proceeding of the Eighth International Conference on Information Quality, 2003.

Gertz, M., Ozsu, M., Saake, G. and Satterler, K. *Data Quality on the Web*, SIGMOD Record, Vol. 33, No. 1, March 2004, pp. 127-132.

Government Accounting Office (GAO). *The Global Information Grid and Challenges Facing Its Implementation*. Washington, D.C.: United States Government, July 2004.

---------. *Recent Campaigns Benefited from Improved Communications and Technology, but Barriers to Continued Progress Remain*. Washington, D.C.: United States Government, June 2004.

---------. *Steps Needed to Ensure Interoperability of Systems that Process Intelligence Data*. Washington, D.C.: United States Government, March 2003.

Government Accounting Office (GAO). *Weaknesses in DoD's Process for Certifying C4I Systems' Interoperability*. Washington, D.C.: United States Government, March 1998.

Haughton, D., Robert, M., Senne, L. and Gada, V. *Effects of Dirty Data on AnalysisResults*, Proceedings of the Eight International Conference on Information Quality, 2003, pp. 64-79.

Horrey, W. and Wickens, C. *Supporting Situational Assessment Through Attention Guidance: A Cost-Benefit and Depth of Processing Analysis*, Proceeding of the 45th Annual Meeting of the Human Factors and Ergonomics Society, Santa Monica, California, 2001.

Information Assurance Technical Framework Forum (IATFF). *Information Assurance for the Tactical Environment*, IATFF Document 3.1, Chapter 9, September 2002.

Irvine, C. and Levin, T. *Quality of Security Service*, ACM, 2001, pp. 91-99.

Joppe, M. *The Research Process*. http://www.ryerson.ca/~mjoppe/ResearchProcess/ accessed 15 March 2006.

Koch, N. "Action Research: Lessons Learned From a Multi-Iteration Study of Computer-Mediated Communication in Groups," *IEEE Transactions on Professional Communications*, Vol. 46, No. 2., 2 June 2003, pp. 105-128.

Koch, N., Chairperson. *IS Action Research: Can We Serve Two Masters?*, Panel 8 discussion at the 1999 International Conference on Information Systems, Charlotte, North Carolina, 12-15 December 1999.

Kuperman, G., Whitaker, R. and Brown, S. *"Cyber Warrior": Information Superiority Through Advanced Multi-Sensory Command and Control Technologies*, IEEE, 2000.

Lipson, H. and Fisher, D. *Survivability – A New Technical and Business Perspective on Security*, Proceedings of the 1999 New Security Paradigms Workshop, Ontario, Canada, September 1999.

Maconachy, W., Schou, D., Ragsdale, D. and Welch, D. *A Model for Information Assurance: An Integrated Approach*, Proceeding of the 2001 IEEE, Workshop on Information Assurance and Security, West Point, NY, 5-6 June 2001.

Majkic, Z. "A General Framework for Query Answering in Data Quality-based Cooperative Information Systems," *ACM*, 2004, pp. 44-50.

Maletic, J. and Marcus, A. *Data Cleansing: Beyond Integrity Analysis*, 5th International Conference on Data Quality, Cambridge, MA, 20-22 October 2000.

Matthews, M., Pleban, R., Endsley, M. and Strater, L. *Measures of Infantry Situational Awareness for a Virtual MOUT Environment*, Proceedings of the Human Performance, Situational Awareness and Automation: User Centered Design for the New Millennium Conference, October 2000.

McEvilley, M. *The Essence of Information Assurance and Its Implications for the Ada Community*, ACM, 2002, pp. 33-39.

Merlo, J., Wickens, C. and Yeh, M. *Effects of Reliability on Cue Effectiveness and Display Signaling*, Army Research Lab Technical Report ARL-99-4, May 1999.

Michael, J., Sibley, E. and Littman, D. "Integration of Formal and Heuristic Reasoning as a Basis for Testing and Debugging Computer Security Policy," *ACM*, 1993, pp. 69-75.

Missier, P. and Batini, C. *A Multidimentional Model for Information Quality in Cooperative Information Systems*, Proceedings of the Eighth International Conference on Information Quality, 2003, pp. 25-40.

Motro, A. "Integrity = Validity + Completeness," *ACM Transactions on Database Systems*, Vol. 14, No. 4, December 1989, pp. 480-502.

Motro, A., Anokhin, P., and Acar, A. *Utility-based Resolution of Data Inconsistencies*, International Workshop on Information Quality in Information Systems, Paris, France, June 2004.

Muncaster, G. and Krall, E. "An Enterprise View of Defensive Information Assurance," *IEEE*, May 1999.

Myers, M. D. "Qualitative Research in Information Systems," *MIS Quarterly*, Vol. 21, No. 2, June 1997, pp. 241-242, updated version, last modified 26 July 2005 www.qual.auckland.ac.nz accessed 15 March 2006.

National Institute of Science and Technology (NIST). *Guide for the Security Certification and Accreditation of Federal Information Systems*, Special Publication 800-37, Gaithersburg, Maryland, May 2004.

National Institute of Science and Technology (NIST). *Recommended Security Controls for Federal Information Systems*, Special Publication 800-53, Gaithersburg, Maryland, February 2005.

---------. *Threats to Computer Systems,* Computer Systems Laboratory Bulletin, Gaithersburg, Maryland, March 1994.

---------. *Security Issues in Public Access Systems,* Computer Systems Laboratory Bulletin, Gaithersburg, Maryland, May 1993.

Office of Management and Budget (OMB). *Management of Federal Information Resources,* Circular No. A-130, Transmittal Memorandum No. 4. Washington, D.C.: United States Government, 28 November 2000.

Orr, K. "Data Quality in Systems," *Communications of the ACM*, Vol. 41, No. 2, February 1998, pp. 66-71.

Perry, W., Signori, D., and Boon, J. *Exploring Information Superiority: A Methodology for Measuring Quality of Information and Its Impact on Shared Awareness*, RAND Corporation, Santa Monica, CA, 2004.

Phillips, C., Ting, T. and Denurjian, S. *Information Sharing and Security in Dynamic Coalitions*, ACM, 2002, pp. 87-96.

Pierce, E. "Assessing Data Quality with Control Matrices," *Communications of the ACM*, Vol. 47, No. 2, February 2004, pp. 82-86.

Redman, T. "The Impact of Poor Data Quality on a Typical Enterprise." *Communications of the ACM*, Vol. 41, No. 2, February 1998, pp. 79-82.

Sage, A. *Systems Engineering*, Wiley-IEEE, 1992.

Sibley, E. and Fry, J. "Evolution of Data-Base Management Systems*," *Computer Surveys*, Vol. 8, No. 1, March 1976, pp. 7-42.

Sterns, R. and Dobson, J. "How Responsible Modeling Leads to Security Requirements," *ACM*, 1993, pp. 143-149.

Strong, D., Lee, Y. and Wang, R. "Data Quality in Context," *Communications of the ACM*, Vol. 40, No. 5, May 1997, pp. 103-110.

Susman, G. and Evered, R. "An Assessment of the Scientific Merits of Action Research" *Administrative Science Quarterly*, 23, 1978.

Tayi, G. and Ballou, D. Editors. "Examining Data Quality," *Communications of the ACM*, Vol. 41, No. 2, February 1998, pp. 54-57.

Turn, R. *Security and Privacy Requirements in Computing*, IEEE, 1986, pp. 1106-1114.

United States Code. *Defense Information Assurance Program.* 12 July 2005.

Wang, R. "A Product Perspective on Total Data Quality Management." *Communications of the ACM*, Vol. 41, No.2, February 1998, pp. 58-65.

Wang, R., Kon, H., and Madnick, S. *Data Quality Requirements Analysis and Modeling*, Ninth International Conference on Data Engineering, Vienna, Austria, April 1993.

Whitehead, J. "Creating a living educational theory from questions of the kind, How do I improve my practice?" *Cambridge Journal of Education*, Vol. 19, No.1, 1989, pp. 41-52

Wulf, W., Wang, C., and Kienzle, D. *A New Model of Security for Distributed Systems*, Computer Science Technical Report CS-95-34, University of Virginia, 10 August 1995.